MW01598395

BRAIDED SKIN

BRAIDED SKIN

Poems | Chelene Knight

MOTHER TONGUE PUBLISHING LIMITED

Salt Spring Island B.C. Canada

MOTHER TONGUE PUBLISHING LIMITED
290 Fulford-Ganges Road
Salt Spring Island, B.C. V8K 2K6 Canada
www.mothertonguepublishing.com
Represented in North America by Heritage Group Distribution.

Copyright © 2015 Chelene Knight. All Rights Reserved. The use
of any part of this publication reproduced, transmitted in any form
or by any means, electronic, mechanical, photocopying, recording
or otherwise, or stored in a retrieval system, without the prior
written consent of the publisher—or, in case of photocopying or
other reprographic copying, a licence from Access Copyright, the
Canadian Copyright Licensing Agency, info@accesscopyright.ca—
is an infringement of the copyright law.

Book Design by Setareh Ashrafologhalai
Cover painting *Chelene* by Charles Mayrs, 2014, acrylics, inks and
    marker pen on paper, 8½" × 10¼"
Typefaces used are Fournier MT and Mr Eaves Sans
Printed on Enviro Cream, 100% recycled.
Printed and bound in Canada.

Mother Tongue Publishing gratefully acknowledges the assistance
of the Province of British Columbia through the B.C. Arts Council
and we acknowledge the support of the Canada Council for the
Arts, which last year invested $157 million in writing and publishing
throughout Canada. Nous remercions de son soutien le Conseil des
Arts du Canada, qui a investi 157$ millions de dollars l'an dernier
dans les lettres et l'édition à travers le Canada.

Library and Archives Canada Cataloguing in Publication

Knight, Chelene, 1981-, author   Braided skin / Chelene Knight.

Poems. ISBN 978-1-896949-50-5 (pbk.)

    I. Title.

PS8621.N53B73 2015   C811'.6   C2015-900105-6

For my daughter, Desiraye,
and my uncle, Eugene Knight (1962–2009)

TABLE OF CONTENTS

"Each member of the family in his own cell of consciousness, each making his own patchwork quilt of reality collecting fragments of experience here, pieces of information there. From the tiny impressions gleaned from one another, they created a sense of belonging and tried to make do with the way they found each other."

TONI MORRISON *The Bluest Eye*

The Skin

BIG CITY

Next to the dog and the deadbolt
second door on the left,
third floor and climbing.
To a city—
worn out from comings and goings.

I danced on hot cement
before you ever knew how.
I was beautiful before too.
Now, like rhythmic breathing, I bring rain.

I've stolen babies from their mothers.
I've changed the world more than once.
I've felt my skin tear quickly—
it healed while I watched.

I rip hearts from trees,
bury them in dirt caves
and watch blades of grass slice soil.

I run blindfolded in the park,
barefoot sometimes too.
I dream nightly in noise.
Big City fuss.
Rushing heels, coffee stained leather,
handbags filled with everything and nothing—
needing it all at once.
I expand the lungs, pulse the blood back.

Swoosh lavender strokes on gold-dipped bellies,
flick neon lights in black corners.

I bring this city back
to life.

BRAIDED SKIN

Let me taste the Ugandan skyline where my father first
opened his eyes—Kampala. Let me touch the deep Southern
roots of my mother, where she first opened her eyes—El Paso.
Sun hits angled glass, spitting confusion into dark eyes, mean
eyes, tired eyes. Eyes of different cities. My skin holds shades
that change when the weather is good. Skin that carries stories
of missing middles, skin that asks questions, questions that
never get answered. No one told me about his journey of
fear-soaked bodies. No one told me where I first opened *my*
eyes. No one kept pictures of sugary days spent melting, hot,
dripping cones of summer. Where did my heart learn to wrap
cloth? Where did my hands learn to paint skin with ink? I
taught myself how to dance on carpets of pond lilies, how
to slip into dresses with braided sleeves, how to braid thick
hair, how to braid thick damp hair—and how to unbraid hair.
They say I am aftershocks, pieces left behind. I am tucked
under sleeves, hidden between skin folds, and under finger-
nails. I rest between loose feathers of outlet jackets. Existing
only on warm lips, cold days and visible breath. I whisper, *I
haven't learned to smile yet.*

THOSE DEVIL EYES, MAMA

i
Sweat wakes me from a fit.
Better leave me be!
I scream this aloud
to no one.

Can't leave this I AM mindset:
This dreamless existence.
Thisbreathlessstate.

Mama, can we talk . . . ?

ii
Remember the worry?
The worry 'bout you chasin'
the night air, thick winds
wrap your thighs—eyes
walkin' and searchin'
for a lil' something to feed
two mouths
while yours went dry and hungry.

My mind sighs—

Mama.

Remember when you
left us, in the night?

6

Those men you brought back
looked at me with devil eyes?
Those devil eyes, Mama.

I know you did things.
Covered your cuts with ripped cloth
from my clean T-shirts that hung on the line.

Sometimes I wonder.
Sometimes I wonder
how you felt in those moments, Mama.
Those moments with the men.

What did you say
when his dry lips moved toward yours?
Did your skin cry?
Did you feel like you were numb, left limp
and that God blessed you
with the inability to feel?

Mama,
did your stomach
jump into your throat
when that man—
that man with the devil eyes
touched your skin?

Sometimes, Mama,
I close my eyes and picture
what inside out must look like.
Wet webs, weaved and hugging.
I leave them where they lay.
I see my face in the sheen
glistening off my heart
as it changes position
in my chest.

Mama, I was seven.
I knew the things you did.
You covered our ears
with your own silent screams,
you hid in a brown paper bag
every night.

I found it on the counter, Mama.
Don't worry.
I can hide.
I can hide real good, Mama.
I won't let the devil eyes,
those devil eyes
will never
see me.

COTTON CANDY

She looks through drawers, shuffles papers, tossing things
aside, like old stamps and folded-up business cards—
searching. Seems like she's always searching. Through her
almost-closed bedroom door, a scream cracks in from Mama,
who's doin' dishes in the kitchen: *It ain't in there!* But she
keeps searching, digging, eyes wide knowing if she blinks,
she'll miss something. She needs to find it. That letter. That
letter from her daddy. The only letter that came. The letter
where he spoke in an unheard-of tongue, where words swam
in and out, side to side and then in a fast, circular motion like
cotton candy spinning on paper cones, translucent at first then
bulking up, pretty pink and puffy. That letter that said things
like *destiny, spectacular* and *regrettably resisting obligations.*
That letter that said ... no, admitted wrong doing and she
needed it. She needed it. Sweat raced down her face in shifts.
There she stood—still, wondering what this hole was she was
trying so hard to fill. A cavity without a bottom. *To let go.*
Realizing it wasn't there, she allowed herself to let go 'cause
like Mama said, *dead leaves that fall won't ever go back home.*
Some things don't need to be found. Let 'em stay lost. She opens
the bottom drawer and in it sits a pen and a lined yellow pad
of paper. In the room with the rummaged-through drawers,
and the almost-closed bedroom door, she writes a letter...

DEAR CURRENT OCCUPANT, APARTMENT ON CLARK DRIVE, ABOVE THE CONVENIENCE STORE

The outside's been painted, but it still looks the same. The same dingy blinds hung there 20 years ago. The tattoo parlour below used to be a convenience store. I wonder about the inside. Have you changed it much? Had my own room there. Had my own door there. Wrote so many sad poems there. Moved everything in using a shopping cart. Twenty-eight back-and-forth trips balancing shelves on top of boxes. One hand for balance, the other for cart-pushing. It was OK though, we got it done. There was a little girl next door. Gave her my old backpack with the yellow and green lightning bolts on it. She was happy. Reminds me of Lauryn Hill. She was ten years old. I had a window in my room that faced a busy street, and the traffic light was right outside that window. People would look up while waiting for the flash from red to green. I'd smile. Didn't have a yard. Didn't need one. Had a big kitchen. No kitchen table. Didn't need one. What do you think about this place? Did you paint the walls? Do you have a family? Sorry about the hole in my bedroom door. My bro threw a Vaseline jar, and I slammed my door just in time. We laughed a lot there. My cousin always came over, danced in my bro's room. *Fresh Prince of Bel-Air* and Lloyd Robertson always on the TV. You know, only had channel 3 and 8. It was sweet when the Rita MacNeil Christmas Special came on 'cause I used to bug my bro, "Hey, there's your girlfriend!" He'd get mad! Oohhhh he'd get so mad haha! We were kids. But you know, things are OK now. Better. Makes me wonder why I'm writing this letter to you. I don't even know you. But now, you know a little bit 'bout me. Not much, but a little.

SECRET LIFE

I can't protect her.

I refuse to build armies
of pigtailed Barbies
with camouflaged faces.

I refuse to wait in bushes
hollow stomach
souring from cigarette smoke.

I refuse to interpret words
whispered in code through door cracks
and thick towels she shoves underneath—
smoke blockers.

I refuse to smell irons.
Hot pressin' devil dresses
she wears to get noticed.

I refuse to listen
to her humming, takin' orders
when wheels slow, she bends at car windows.

I refuse to protect her.
White eyes set
off black leather shadows.

I refuse to hold her body
that shivers after nightmares
of cement-covered strawberries,

shriveled tangerines
and human-eyed birds.

I refuse to keep her secret.

They've got her.

AS A MATTER OF FACT

If you use slang, use it.
Do not put on airs—join a select society.
Space the page.
Leave a blank question mark
to the round-the-island race.

Become one:
Bedchamber
Wildlife
Bellboy
(Play tricks on the sounds.)

Ask it to cast its spell over words.
Righthand, lefthand.
Rough width?
Exception?
Accommodate this
expression punctuated by itself.
A rocky uneven bottom
unfit for anchorage,
enclosed in your heart
'til it stops beating.

I can't attend.

A coffin is a small domain
far from the crowd.

An alphabetical list
at the end,
in the second scene
of the third act
placed under guard.
                    Divided.
The student will examine the pages of any carefully printed book.

UGANDA 1972

A once promising land—evaporating. The people abolished,
divided and shaken by the expulsion, the elimination. The threat
of an ethnic cleansing of the Indian minority hovered over

Asian carpenters, mechanics, shoemakers and tailors—the
middlemen flail in the political winds. Minority eyes must speak:
Identify yourself; breakthrough for Uganda.

Kampala—tombs of *kabakas* have woven thatched roofs that
swoop to a point high above the straw-laden floors, lending a
cathedral-like silence to the sacredness of the earth below

where royal attendants continually watched over the remains
of their dead kings. Kampala—the arched and pillared windows
were endless.

Nestled behind sundown, rests an Indian dialect of silks and
cottons. Their eyes lettered names like "Patel," "Desai" and
"Bombay Emporium."

The ashes of Uganda walked many miles and carried their heads.
The walk was tedious work.

It took years. Now, it's an image left behind.
Why should we wait in line for justice?

*Help us begin to drink the pain of Uganda, and one day replant our
roots.* The mountains appear at sunset, and the hillsides of women
flow in the breeze.

The men bring comfort, but their eyes tell stories of death.
In their minds, their birth. Precious jewels in a hairdo or
turban—confiscated, but still hear tales of escape.

They look back on the homes they built. They look back
on the tiny store their grandfather established. Alone in
their difficult hours.

Uprooted.

THE MISUSE OF HOSTILE ACTS

i
Feature the replacement of one word:
                        Re
place

the shape in question.
Irritate familiar speech.

An unreal image flooded them,
cut down the market
(by buying stock perhaps).

Anybody?
Anyone?
Any single thing?

My opinion is sufficient—
The best dancer in the club
unprepared for war.

ii
Hostile acts may be used.
Mammals, reptiles and birds.
First as soldier,
and second, administrator.

Contact people:
- Look them up
- Phone them
- Find them
- Meet them

Not to be misused
but an apple is composed of seeds,
flesh and skin.
Pale green
melts at a certain temperature.

Deciding battles
adds nothing in saving lives.
Combustable?
Think trucks carrying
gasoline or explosives.
Concerned with the safety of children?
Limited to chance.

iii
It is silly to say
"free-floating."
It offends the ear.
The erosion leads
to softness or nonsense.

Tell the story without error.
Restrict it to its fossil resin.
Its defenders dead
with fatigue.

Lend me your ears!
We are improving in many ways.
Hostile acts should be avoided
unless the reader cannot tell.

No one will save me.

I will drown
in the new-fallen snow
on the porch.

STOLEN SEEDS

From beginning to end,
too deeply rooted to be taken
from inside, from me.
A whole season breezes—
without wanting or willing
to ask me to speak.

Fearful if I don't choose, and so
I speak for you both.
In turn I am burdened
with the weight
of two thousand pounds
of unused blank pages.

I open my mouth,
words come out as clouds—
magenta and melon, fading, somber.
Black rain and blurred everything.
My enemy—
matches my regret with his smirk.

I hide behind my shadow,
duck behind pillars of unnamed flesh.

I want to be somewhere else.
Someone else.

Gone are the days when the wind
chose my face to brush against.
I'm a stranger
flailing in a pool of muddy water.
Cracked tea cups float around me.

The garden motions to me to come back.
She wraps me in green
and sinks my hands in the dirt again.

IF BUGS COULD TALK

Every year we send stories:
Share them.
Remember.
Visit.
Flip the details.

Find love on the #3 bus.

For the first time
I sit in the fold,
accordion-like, available.

Three stops to talk,
exchange courage.

I chase days, bend sound.

Plan on running?
From Germany,
from the Prairies
and fall

    deep.

IN THE GREEN ROOM

i

Eyes on me. Long stare up and down. Longer stare. Stuck in this frustrating and degrading conversation. You—who won't be happy with the answer I give because your perception of blackness is completely distorted. Assumptions come to the table already orally armed. Defend my skin tone, hair colour, hair length and hair texture. Isn't this one of the most multi-cultural-mixed-biracial-baby-breeding cities in the world? And no—you cannot touch my hair.

ii
Tangled. Caught between
nails of acrylic tips.
Rows
of fish tails
intertwine—

A maintained fusion.

Cut dead ends
then weave these tracks
back like
braids and plaits.
She oils
and slicks sides,
pats down then poofs up—

Make up your mind.

One drop rule bleeds
into the blue-eyed illusion of
good hair.
Stressed to over-process
these tips,
these roots,
these plaits,
these locks—
        She dreads.

Enter.
Stage left,

and find the mic . . .

iii
Sing sweet.
These brown skin confessions.
Brown skin,
black skin,
caramel-dipped skin,
leathery-sunburnt skin,
ceases-to-remember skin,
like the war-torn-country skin,
she breathes—
skin.

Found fourteen feathers
in a notebook.
Imprinted on
creased pages.
Faded cover
lead to
an ellipsis.

Watched eyes burn holes
through layers
of skin
        yet
never happy
with these answers of ethnicity.
Let's gather confessions
of ebony-boned

princesses.
Let's steal stories of

brown-skinned contessas
and drown memories of
her one-tone-let-me-pick-a-side—

      Skin.

The Voice Inside Her Hair

"Adults, older girls, shops, magazines, newspapers, window signs—all the world had agreed that a blue-eyed, yellow-haired, pink-skinned doll was what every girl child treasured. 'Here,' they said, 'this is beautiful, and if you are on this day 'worthy' you may have it.'"
TONI MORRISON *The Bluest Eye*

i

What do you think about this colour, Mama? Feel the fabric between your fingers. Do you think this shade of blue makes my eyes pop? What about my hair? Does it look the same as it looked when you used to do it Sunday mornings? I miss sitting on the porch with you while you pulled and pulled and pulled my hair. I hid the pain when I saw your face gleam under the hot sun. You had that shiny, deep brown skin, just like mine. I been trying every day, Mama. I iron my dresses the night before and hang 'em just like you showed me, and look, I got creases too! I don't want 'dem girls at school throwing their words at me again. I don't know why they say I am a bad shade of brown, I don't get it, Mama. I have been trying to show them, and I have been trying to show you, I'm beautiful.

ii

Mama, I'm older now. Listen.

Forget beauty, too many years have passed, we are *still* not people in the eyes of the paper bag rule: Light skin and dark

skin divided. (Men on women) We want: Light skinned, long
hair. (Women on men) We are: Imprisoned within our own
tangled web—We Weave. I breathe the day, Mama, when the
shades of brown and black won't matter. Mothers should be
teachin' daughters, we are not our hair or our skin. Why wasn't
skin colour always a thing of pride? The palms of hands, and
the soles of feet like ribbons of creamed silk on coffee. We are
not the pieces of the broken things inside.
We are not *on* the outside.

iii
Sometimes, Mama, I feel like my hair speaks to me in bursts . . .

Exit the stage. Release me now. See how quick curls unwind?
Coils fall to graze soft, cocoa shoulders. Don't be scared,
go ahead and admire your reflection smiling back off that
magenta-lipstick-kissed glass. It's yours. Copper eyes heavy,
holding, carrying. Remember those eyes? Before, you sat
folded. Knees kissing jewelled lips, arms around bony brown
legs—watched rivers bend. Saw water trickle down the sun's
edge—threaded it with light. You were willing to withstand
the pain, willing to endure burn sores, the smell of permed hair
and the hole in your pocket. Ask yourself: without it,
can you still sing sweet? Everybody around you says your skin
changes colour in the dark, everybody asks questions, every-
body says something: Who does your hair like that?

Dusting leads to finger waves and flat twists. You won't see

—a demarcation line—

as I transition
this hair,
I wrap.

Natural hair, more personal than political. The usual once-a-
week ritual of Sunday hair washing in a semi-grip between
Mama's knees, painfully comb, section, oil, plait—protect the
pain with a sharp smack to the knuckles with the comb. The
pain was always well groomed for special occasions, tied with
matching ribbons. We never *spoke* of hair.

iv

In your hair journey from childhood to your epiphany as
a Black Woman, your experience contained detail. Natural
curly hair—straightened. When you begin your walk to and
through self over and over again, it is difficult to go against the
grain. Mama taught you hair is statement, but you were too
young to look like a rebel, too young to choose. Permission
to wear an Afro? Pin up dreadlocks? Your first image was all
over the news. Amazing Afro. You didn't know the politics.
Visions of a raised fist entered your vocabulary. Hide beauty?
Permission granted. Whispers: Your roots must be redone
every two weeks.

Face the mirror. What is beautiful?
Look now:
Hair growth, new roots, follicles that will not L(y)e
flat.   Picture that.

The Music

LIFELINE

Pulse
the beat back . . .
like Nina, I wanna
little sugar in my bowl
with cinnamon sunsets
that rest at the sound of her.

Pulse
the beat back . . .
O Lady Day let me taste this strange fruit, but Lauryn,
questions the denial of its roots.
Honey-coated-throat-whispers
say time to get free—
Coltrane compose for me.
Beloved Afro blue and lush life.

She's a gold-back-hustla.
Rhyme for a dollar?
Breath of anise.
She's mine.
Dance for me?
A dime.
Or she
sings maybe
just for me
and she
seals the cracks in my armour.

A beat, pulse the blood back.
lyrical intravenous—
pulse
the blood back . . .

Never belonging. Never fitting. Always watching things
happen through cold, frosted windows. Windows caked with
years of dust that never seemed to get clean, even when Mama
was dead-set on scrubbin'—the dust remained. The smell
remained. This house remained. This window was the blurred
lens through which he saw life. This was how he saw his
mother change shape. James, 13 years old, sat cross-legged
outside on the porch of the small, white shed-like house that
he and his mother shared. Their house. Their treasures. Their
everyday things. Their lives. This house—the siding peeling,
faded and mismatched, unrecognizable as white, dingy-grey
at best—held them together. The porch had the worst fate.
The boards, each one loose and most of them rotted. James
knew the exact ones to walk on to not fall through. He made
a game of it, marked the "good" floor boards with bright red
*X*s. Jumped from one red *X* to another to get inside the house
without the porch caving in. James sat alone on the porch
quite often. His preference. Alone with his paper, colouring
book and favourite extra-sharp pencil. He liked to keep the
No. 2 HB Paper Mate Classic behind his ear. *I look like a pro.*
He drew anything and everything. He was particular about
the shading of things, getting that darkness or lightness just
right. *It's all about the pressure.* He worked on his self-portrait.
His self. *Press harder where you want to create shadow.* His
thoughts interrupted by the daily right-on-time-high-pitched-
sound-of-muffled-demands-exploding-through-the-screen-
door. Hearing Mama's screams from inside the house, he

quickly hides his drawing and his HB Paper Mate pencil under a loose floorboard. Heads inside.

Outsider.

HEALING NEVER AT ALL

The air outside the church is heavy and thickens with the sound of the choir, these church hollers hitting notes that carry all the way out to the street, where he stands. Staring into the window, he sees large brown arms shooting into the air—flailing and swinging and praying. Then, the face of his Mama pierces right back at him through the glass.

Over the hollers of the church folk, she speaks to him in slow motion through stained glass expecting him to read her lips, and those lips shake like index fingers in the face—shaming him for being there and not being there, for breathing wrong, for wearing those black pants with the elastic waist, for leaving the milk out, for not saying yes ma'am, for not saying no ma'am, and she said he would go to hell because the faithless live there. He asks her where hell is, and her lips shake like fingers again. He looks away.

City noise takes over. Cars whizzing by, ignoring traffic signs and lights, while horns blare and the wind whips his ears with freezing whispers. She exits the church and walks toward him.

He swallows and looks down at his feet pretending to kick a pebble, anything to avoid her gaze, but eventually he looks up. Her houndstooth jacket makes him dizzy, the shoulders over-padded, the pockets empty, and the collar opens just enough for the wind to sneak in. A cough escapes. Loud enough it forces him to swing his head back to look at what or who

could make such a noise, and he closes his eyes and wonders
about stained glass, faith and hell.

She walks away.

Standing alone on the curb, alone with the swirling of the
silence, spinning his whole body in every direction.

She left him in this city, and the lights spoke, o-shaped-
daybreak noise. *Oh Lord,* he says to himself, looks down
at pants worn at the knees, *carry me home safe.* He walks,
glancing at the smiling faces that pass him, he looks back at
them, only with his eyes, never lifting his head, being careful
not to meet their gaze. Hands in his thin pockets, he walks, he
feels a coin in his pocket and grips it tight, he walks. He sees a
park bench across the street in front of Aunt Maggie's Press n'
Curl. *Maybe I will wait for Mama here.* He sits.

Healing never at all.

Hands still in thin pockets, a coin still tightly gripped, still
thinking about stained glass, faith and hell, still dizzy from
Mama's houndstooth jacket and the shaking finger-like lips,
he smiles. He sees her down the street, bags in hand, and
her shadow, her outline, her image gets clearer as she strides
toward him. Traffic noise lessens to a dull hum, and the
ringing in his head dims out slow then fast. Like the quick
flick of a light switch, he opens his eyes, and she's standing
there, and he wonders for how long.

QUICK BREAD DREAM

It started with the bread being stale. Rushed cooking. Rushed eating. They were done before I could serve myself. Now, everything is a mess. He calls a cab. I didn't see him call, but he announces its arrival. *Sometimes those cabs take two hours it seems*. He's antsy. He wants to hurry. I scramble to gather our things. Things we would need for an overnight trip. I can't find anything. The house gets messier. I'm flicking light switches, turning the stereo and TV off then on. Looking for clothes and my phone. It's taking too long. He seems relieved. I change my mind. He sighs. The house is a disaster. The kids seem shorter, younger. I hear drums pounding outside the door echoing through the neighbourhood. Finally I'm ready. I go back in to turn off another light. He's yelling now. He seems so different. What's changed? It doesn't matter. I'm too late. He pushes past me. Running. I watch as he opens the car door and climbs in. I open my mouth to scream, but no sound comes out. The cab speeds off. I'm left standing alone in my doorway, bags in hand; it's quiet now.

BETTER OFF

I wake up
my breath is snagged
on pieces you left behind.
Unwashed T-shirts frame the floor.
Morning's toast crumbs
set up camp on my round black table.

Surrounded by decisions
like whether or not to drink
the three-day-old coffee
or scrub the brown sludge
off the inside of a cold unused oven.
My mouth and throat burn
with the rancid oil taste of daily routine

My clothes don't fit the same today.
You were right.
Folded flesh ain't cute.

Never met Perfection,
But I've been close friends with Good Enough.
Cling to a feeling
that hangs willingly on the line to dry
held by two loose clips.

Listen with my eyes first
as trees glide for me

outside my small window—
All I have left.

There's no wind in sight.

SHEDS WINGS ON MONDAY MORNINGS

Every woman has purpose.
Standing on a precipice—nothing.
No, at the moment *I* was
at my end—
loss had made me.

I came to feel for things.

life just . . .

My mother died . . .

I had scarcely . . .

no longer young.

Black room of this—
tells me she's a coded lyric.
There was nothing.
Things of loss.
This life I had

I had never seen, never known
and was always
less of someone.

Between me,
between myself.

Realization at my back.
So for my beginning,
beginning of time.
In abundance.

Too much sugar in my biscuits.
Came to me: Look!
And more of?
Had it all.
Realized.

White stain lines remain 'til midday,
in the whole, and eternity.
Whose face, a bleak, black—
been used.
A self-proclaimed couch warrior.

Whole life standing,
this would lay genius
on sun-worn arm rests.
My life.
The wind.

For this woman,
wears a black robe,
crooked balance.
Know this.
I,

only my,
wings shed on Monday mornings.

A WOMAN'S TOUCH

Sit down on some topic.
The sounds of hesitant bursts in between,
get stuck in an awkward tangle.
Overblown—
Why can't I get this right?

This quiet book, like a wall sampler.
Unblock my web!
Condition a feminine female farmer,
out of the box, to touch
the sweet
almost perfect thought.

SATURDAY NIGHT AT CALABASH

Think crisp white.
Pants creased and thin-lined
like the whites of eyes slit back.

Music flows—
Steady now, bend backs to this,
this rhythm, watch now
as her staccato tics and tocs
shake like she owns this song:

Long time no see.
Baby watch me,
now watch this
then swing with me,
and dream baby dream.

Louder now, coconut drinks splash her chin.
She grins within that steamy-hot
corner of the darkest-of-dark spots.

In this heat, this blazing,
a line of white glows and moves with hips.

Speak that foreign tongue.

Her eyes look up at starlight's last words:

44

This is the place
where broken stars
close their eyes
to dream.

Her lips speak of blue-rose and jasmine.
Her legs move like air-filled tunnels to nowhere.
High heels and clenched purse strings.
She has this need,
this need to be noticed 'n' she dances—

She dances like flames could lick the sky.

THE UN-WIFE

I warned her.
But there she stands,
waiting to be
some foolish man's wife.

I told her.

Don't need to
crease collars or kiss cold cheeks at night.
Don't need to
rinse plates or red paint those lips
to hide the swell of her eye and the black of her ribs.

Not me.

I shake rooms in silence,
heels clicking
swerve chairs, spin heads
like highway accidents,

I reminded her.

Don't need to impress:
• with granite countertops,
• rings of promises,
• imported fortresses

I definitely ain't no hostess.

I sing to myself.

Honey-lined eyelids, dream sweet, now I can reminisce.
I need deep v-neck polo shirts purple in hue,
I need soul, steady groove,
Thick brown espresso-rimmed demitasse.

I watch now,
as she slips into her tough new skin.

I'll miss her.

HOW TO RUN YOUR FINGERS THROUGH MY HAIR
For Craig Brewer

Everyone has to contribute a verse. Get it down on paper,
on tape, on canvas, on napkin, on palms of hands or on a
crumpled-up grocery receipt, get it down. Speak in prose,
encrypted simplicity, and wrap words around words like hands
wrap thighs. Let brown eyes drink the blue fragrance of voice.
Dream that fragrance. Learn. By any means necessary. Tell
stories. Tell tales of all the mamas combin' daughter's hair.
Every morning. Preach that pain, that tightness, that jaw-
clenching fierceness that eventually—causes numbness. Look
up, see the light even when it hurts to smile, for days and days
and days at a time. Remember stories of hair. *Your* stories. Talk
'bout that separate entity, that journey. What's *my* contribution?
I'll answer questions: "Do you braid? Do you do slack plaits?
You quick? Where you from?" Let me tell you where I'm from:
I'm from my softness, my texture, my smoothness, my smile.
I am from my words, my syntax, my mama's skin-burnin' hot
wax, and I'm from myself. I'm from my hair, my stories—
pulled, stretched, curled, loose strands balled up and tossed; I
am from every last piece of every last breath—taken and given.
I will tell stories, share stories and write stories. By any means
necessary. So, you wanna run your fingers through my hair?

THE SWAY OF MY JEWELLED BACK POCKETS

Skin shivering like the tingle
of sweet peppermint tea.
Caressing cheeks—
tongue ripples.

Orange ink sails
down patterned forearms.
Travels down long spines,
spreads then stops
at lower back
finding hips—
gripping.

I am deeply wedged
between my conscience and you.
Then finally, I'm like ice—
            slick and sliding
between your warm fingertips.
Skin speaks,
curls,
stops—
then thaws.

Your fingerprints left on me
like evidence
on countertops—
            Permanent.

My body's only song,
conveniently hidden in the sway
of my jewelled back pockets.

My intentions slip
into a bed of bravado
roll onto the floor
next to walls
pulsing . . .
bass
through
speaker wire—

NEW VOICE OF AN OLD PHOTO

Camera raw.
364 shades of brown laid out—
for toning and hand colouring.
You call my body:
"The Snapshot Chronicles."

Gradient light (adjusted).
Mixed emulsions slipping
just like the albumen and salted paper.
You're skilled at this filter exposure—
Expose me.

You lead me into a dark room
step by step
(basic development).
Polaroid manipulations
laugh in the life of a writer.

Your laugh is like braided shadows—
Dark. Eyes on me.
You say I am like a practical director
from a $30 film school—basic.
Shutters click, fast then slow.

You weave me between the light.
Paint me grey in between the seconds and minutes.
Time passes. We travel backwards.
Before, we spoke of braiding.

Unlikely strands unravelling beneath
other unlikely strands,
endless unfolding.

My hands left to do the work
of the empty.

A MUSICIAN DREAMS IN NOVEMBER

People are always late in November.
Midnight dreary, damp tree leaves gather,
they sit quiet with abandon.
We did not go; *they* have gone.

Moths swarm around a burning candle.
They wanted to get even,
conquer the world.

When it gets dark, colder, we'll find music.
Stand alone as raccoons steal food.

I asked her a question:
"Express the meaning of frayed ribbon?"

"Dancing flowers must be consistent in number."

A solo flute plays
as winter approaches.
She is the leader.
We opened the door,
she went out the window.

Singers, places, cities
matter greatly
as past, present or future.

The freezing wind in an embroidered handkerchief
that indicates whether the guitar was played.

HE IS CHILD

Waiting is like pulling feathers
in slow motion from seams.
Waiting is like ants crawling on heat vents.
Re-routing, leaving scented trails.

She stops to watch him.
He moves quick between cracks of door frames.
He follows patterned sidewalks.
He dodges grooved soles of shoes.
She knows he is genius, he is child.

He leads her to waterfalls pouring from cliffs.
Tips of minds.
Tips of thought.
Tips of stretched veins that block—
Everything starts from something.

Strung like white frosted beads.
The line moves like spiders
that create moist silks
dropped on to broken bottles
that cut soft fingers.

Waiting—watching sequined stars burn out.
Waiting—trails lead to fires with soft blue centres
that burn souls and footsteps of velvet.
She knows he is genius.

LAST KISS GOODNIGHT

Remember the graveyard?
The already prepared holes
we prepared ourselves.
Like Sunday dinner,
gravy boats and untouched Brussels.

I am queen of things left to rot.
To be forgotten and to rust
like metallic lamps in rain—
genies leave warm fingers to rub.
And stupid wishes?
Torn from hands, cities and air.
And corpses?
Stop. They are luckier than us.

Frozen—
like peas and carrots,
they please everyone.
We get to remember
the way they used to feel
when we kissed,
when we hugged,
when we left them tingling.

You hear me speak?
Lucky you. I'm not there yet—
that graveyard.

I leave them gunning: pulled strings,
concussions—
blood rushing—

I smoke backwards.
Chokeholds
cut holes in most
curved spines' flatline.
I get to prepare these holes.
I get to flick dirt.
You lose teeth, crooked smiles.
One side, corner rise.
I put them under.
They can't rise without me.

IF TEETH COULD TALK

In this final hour
the gums numb.
Buttery tongues taste
the blood,
like flavour enhancers.

Sapphire eyes drift
to thoughts—slicing the throats
of evening skies
as cheeks grow round and ruby.
Please suction these rivers
of the microscopic.

Alveolar bone
surrounds the root,
anchors it in place.
Permission granted.
Slice the apex.

Raw on top of raw,
the heavens open—
Go ahead.
Bond my surface.

STRAND 3

The City

BREAKFAST, LUNCH AND DINNER

You have broken in through my sliding door, just off my back-
yard where we used to play tag—three times now. Middle of
the night and with the soft, slow sounds of clicks and flicks,
the latch releases from its housing. Unlocked. I wake.

Why do you rip down the walls, leaving mounds of thick
white dust on my newly vacuumed carpet? What are you
looking for—in those walls? The wooden shelves that I hung
myself in my small bathroom, destroyed. You leave jagged
pieces of the cheap wood

hanging, tilted, angled, sharp.
You hide in the closet for hours and hours at a time. I don't
know how you fit yourself in amongst the towels, toilet paper
stockpile and my daughter's old booster seat

'cause you are probably kneeling there in pain, fighting off
numbness and a slight cramp in your left leg. There's no room
for a body. You nibble on a carrot for sustenance, fuel to keep
you standing—there in my small closet. Three times I have
had to ask questions:

What do you do on your days off? Did you always steal
leather-bound notebooks? What will you tell the police? Two
versions of the same dream, hunger is your excuse for taking
everything that's white: the fridge, stove, dryer.

Three times now, I opened my eyes to the sound of my own
fierce rapid pounding, my awareness agile like animal survival

tactics—a wolf can sneak up behind, but instead his smirk
sings in front of me, changing timbres, hitting notes that
choke me still.

Three times I've patched holes made from your putative exca-
vations. I go to sleep knowing you'll come, I always dream in
threes
and wait—to be fed.

TURNING 19 IN VANCOUVER

Small.
An ideal season.
A solid foundation.

Heavier jasmine?
                Push!—
A flower charms you with its twist.
Blackberry backdrop
made from the nose,
summer,
haze, honey light—mellow moon,

unfiltered.
Create a cloudy finish.

Touch is slight—fresh character,
a two-row
secret mountain
of clove, clean, dry.

Effervescent.

Kick sweet grass!
Highlight the style of German winds
(timeless lift). Inspired by the loaded touch of crystal.

Lighter in style.
A style originated to survive

the sea voyage
to troops serving India.

Soft accent, imported.
Deep amber of ocean,
grass and earth—
use this for balance.
Bitterness is followed by a shock wave, unless otherwise specified.

I CHOOSE A LIFE OF STYLE

In those days, I passed life.
Deposits of gold cut the vast tangle
of a still tiny thing, a barely tarnished gem.

I have been refurbished.
A recent vintage—fresh.
Assault, correct, delete, enliven.

I tried to soften the flavour of discussion.
—Plain style.
Snappin' orders:
Do not join!
Do not break voice!

The bold face:
His steel-rimmed bling,
and carefully edged mustache.
His heart was sitting with such relish!
A man left with nothing to say.

I have been trying to cry every word—

The tight world of quick lessons?

Cut the deadwood.

They learn to trim.
They learn to quiver.

But a shadow seems to hang over you
a thousand times in the heat,
in the cool, in this late season.

Invigorate me.
I am thousands of likes and dislikes.

A displayed body.

Remove the tonsils
Remove the throat—
(the most inflexible of all inflexibilities).

Disregard the rules.
A dusty spirit of a man.
A version of the colourless.

Say it loud!
Say it loud!
The elements floundering in a swamp.
Drain this swamp.
Get up on dry ground.

Today,
to me?
A blessing undisguised.

THE HOME TEAM ADVANTAGE

Pale space dust, bitter and dry.
West Coast love is easy.
It is undoubtedly the West's choice.
Inspired by the rich tradition of the exotic.
(that means Columbus, Chinook and Cascade.)

This *West Coast* Style—
A sumo grand master.

Bring balance.

Vancouver East Side.
Bitter and brilliant
At the end of the boil,
a gentle drift—
                        Victoria B.C.
7% intense and restrained,
5.3% character.
A result of the addition
of 11 pounds of fresh.
deep brown-black body
                        flaked raw.

Is it elusive?
Is it soft on the tongue?
Very complex, the use
of texture, body, *Gypsy Tears*

and a burst
of green.

TEXTBOOK THOUGHTS ESCAPE

Choose to ramble.
A sonnet is more flexible
but skeletons bring the flesh
and the blood.

It holds a single,
short, slight description—
An action.

By itself a signal has been reached.

In dialogue, rapid talk
serves the whole.
Transition the breeze.
Reverse this device, any device.

The heavy lamp emerged on the roof
(animated narrative).

Less direct, less bold, less concise—
Tastes of modern readers.

Dead leaves lying on the ground.
Crowing of a rooster.
Weak in spots.

Shakespeare's works?
A waste of time.

Insignificant?
Negative words smiled on me.
Plath died young.

Your writing will lack authority.
Real uncertainty.

It rained Homer, Dante,
Shakespeare in the zoo.
By the railroad tracks,
red vixen, a deodorized skunk,
a parrot from Tahiti.
Understand!

Never mastered the way to Hell.
Drained it of its blood.
(Orwell's translation)
Taught by the textbook.

The laboratory method.

8:17 AM AT 29TH STATION

Surrounded by wet faces and stretched skin.
Creases tell stories of the night before.
Jam-packed—herded

I look up, read ads to avoid locking eyes
with anyone.
No spot between gripped hands

Place my palm on the ceiling
of the train to stable myself.
Can't fall on these strangers.

Getting out was harder than the game of Jenga
I played to get in. Squeeze my soaked body.
Lost my umbrella.

The sky's sadness drenches me.
Mold could grow on my cheeks.
Severed cords cheaply repaired with dollar store thread.

No point gasping for air—
breath lost amongst the hurried crowds of trench coats.
Bending puzzle pieces, uncomfortably tight.

False security and the sounds of latches and clicks
followed by a tightening of the belt
around my chest.

CHILDREN EAT YOUR BREAD

"Children eat your bread,
little children eat your bread
'cause it all, all falls down.
Telling you all, it all falls down."
LAURYN HILL *"Mystery of Iniquity"*

Children eat your bread.
I'll warm the stove,
pour the milk, butter toast.
Ignore the neighbours' screams.
The sky is falling.

Let's carry conversations
of visible breathlessness.
Children please eat your bread.
Wipe your faces clean.

Get your things ready.
Quiet the television now.
Did you remember to eat your bread?
Get your shoes on.
My fingers are bleeding.

Walk together.
Don't drag your feet.
Your shoes are untied.
Board the bus, three seats in the back.
I wish you had eaten your bread.

Let's take our seats.
The sun will die soon.

Look out the dusty windows.
See those trees and the people's faces?
They didn't eat their bread.
Long ago, they were ordinary people.
The sky's stars will hang themselves.

Ring the bell please.
Our stop is coming up next.
Children is there bread in your pockets?
Quick, push open the door.
                    The air   will eat us now.

I'm telling you all,
it all falls—

down.

HOME REMEDIES

My wings are dull knives
slicing skylines, swallowing air,
falling down onto chipped doorsteps.
She's waiting, cold concrete.
We discuss things we've tried,
things we've done.

Remember the wet leaves
I scooped from mesh bags
and rubbed in severed wings?

Internet advisory!

She's stubborn.
She wedges lemons
between yellow teeth
to kill foul breath.
Sour lies, sour lies!
Squints eyes that eat air.

Tried aloe to soothe raised skin.
It always works in movies.
Those tales of fairies and fairy tails
swoosh like magic, bend metal
and make dishes dance.

Exhale—
shoot into skies again.

Soar—skim   white space.
Those things we've tried,
those things we've done.
My apologies.
I killed the sky.

SPEAK EASY

She eats alone on park benches. She opens her mussels with
switchblades. She has a fierce appetite. She's done things,
rough things, close-your-eyes-in-the-dark things, slice-
thorns-with-skin things. To shake and to swing is easy.
To shake and to swing to the sound of the harmonica being
played by the man down the street is divine. Pigeons follow
her in the dark. They know from the sound of mussels
cracking that she has a fierce appetite. Her voice is raspy when
she's hungry. She eats often. The moon hides. She speaks soft
in daylight. Her voice is whipped air. She wears white dresses
that tickle freshly shaved skin. White dresses, always white
dresses. No pocket for her switchblade. She strings it around
her neck. The sun hides. Pigeons follow her in the dark. They
follow, they always follow. They know from the sound of
mussels cracking, she has a fierce appetite.

Passing through the empty halls, she runs her fingers along the black, charred walls, the stained and peeling wallpaper curls towards her. Walking, her eyes wide, she moves carefully to avoid all the broken furniture and ragged toys around her feet. She swears she hears the wailing of a baby, her sister, red-faced and tight-fisted wishing for the familiar taste of burnt toast and spoiled milk. It was the same scream she hears from her sister when Mama shovels the repulsive Buckley's cough syrup down her throat. Just a memory. "I miss my family." She closes her eyes. Her memories drift to the smell of thick cut bacon Mama would make once a month on a good day when the money came, crushed almonds and brown sugar would melt on her tongue, like clouds of heavy cream. Things were good when the money came, Mama would sing, and the house was clean and smelled of lavender and pine. She stumbles now in her scuffed leather heels. Clanking up the worn wood stairs, hot tears run down her ruby cheeks as she enters the kitchen. The black-and-white checkerboard floor tiles used to gleam when Mama scrubbed them on her hands and knees, now they are covered with thick grey dust and singed wood from what used to be their cupboards. She falls to her knees and sobs. She digs her nails into the floor where she used to play. She thought of Mama in her kitchen, so proud, grinding spices and the scent of cardamom and turmeric. Mama's fried chicken sizzling in her only cast iron skillet. She never once flinched when the hot oil splattered on her skin. She would just flick at it as if it were nothing more

than a tiny coarse black hair and keep flipping the chicken,
swaying, smiling and humming a nameless tune.

A SERIES OF THREE

The ancient temple?
Somebody's error.
There is no defense.

Refuse this fine mess!
The Reverend, the novelist, the poet.
In need of a time or place.

Identify the audience.
Which? When? Where?
           Add something...

Throw stones as Mary sings.
Their possession of the city—
Reconstructed.

One chance of escape.

We cannot reach town.
We cannot reach town.
We cannot reach town?

This simple method,
a dark tomb.   Here:
God disposes.

The bridge fell.
Do not break in two.

A clipped blunder   for broken stars.

     A chapter departs.

The mirror linking

    jar,

jam,

     marbles—

Heavy eaters.
Down the road,
a soldier of the city.

HEAVENS OPEN

His body's killing
the guardian's relief.

Our children's shoes sleep
on shavings—

The women feel it!
In the air, in the eyes.

Empty jars ship themselves
from the sky

and the clouds whip
the city.

The ground will rise up!
For the old man,

his daughter,
her son.

Bloom—
like cotton in a jar of water.

GOLD-PLATED DREAMS

In this final chapter, we leave solid ground. Who can say
words explode in the mind? Who knows why music is thinly
disguised? To shape their steering stars in motion? We speak
on paper. Spirits incognito, talk rhythm by mouth, earth and
teeth. Wooden fingerprints feel weak. The body is slave in
these passages. The evening is like curious, laughing flesh, a
garnish for the meat, a dull dish of devices. The pen becomes
wing shots, the bird flashes by in the background. The child
will echo design of brick and steel. A cathedral took shape
from this airy mountain. The click and flow of leeches infest
the blood of words. Let loose the genius! The breezy work of
the empty. A livelier tongue—one's ear is lustier than intes-
tine. A stomach tickled by a claw. Why? Because it sounds
more violent? Be wild of tongue! Become muddiness on
the highway, rapid-fire illuminating breath. A swordfish in
an hour glass with foreign expression. Gold-plated dreams
inflate like balloons, soon burst in bright sound. Rhyme this
animal—wet with style, she is at home in the rain.

NOTES AND ACKNOWLEDGEMENTS

Braided Skin could not have been written without the insight
and inspiration from my peers and mentors at Simon Fraser
University's The Writer's Studio. I owe a lot of credit to
my mentor, Jen Currin, who saw a spark in my writing and
gave me the opportunity to grow, and the encouragement to
compile this book. I am beyond grateful to book designer,
Setareh Ashrafologhalai for her unique touch, and Mona
Fertig at Mother Tongue Publishing for giving my book
such a good home. A huge thank you to Charles Mayrs for
creating the beautiful book cover painting, and for bringing
my vision to life. Thank you to Jennifer Zilm, Barbara
Baydala and Wayde Compton for being my first readers. My
daughter, Desiraye, has always been, and will always be, my
main motivation to continue writing, and her words, "why
don't you just do your writing, and stop waiting around" will
keep me doing just that. Thank you to my Uncle Eugene for
keeping me on the right path. I miss you everyday.

. . .

"Braided Skin," "Uganda 1972," "Last Kiss Goodnight" and
"Lifeline" (all edited versions) were first published in *Emerge
2013 Anthology.* "In the Green Room" and an edited version
of "A Musician Dreams in November" were first published in
The Raven Chronicles literary magazine. "If Teeth Could Talk"
was first published in *Sassafras Literary Magazine.* "Speak
Easy" was first published in *Room Magazine.*

"Sheds Wings on Monday Mornings" is a chance operations poem using a combination of the first page of *Autobiography of My Mother*, by Jamaica Kincaid, and my own eight-line poem entitled "Sixty-Four." Kincaid's words were cut into words and phrases. My poem was cut into eight separate lines. All the words, phrases and sentences were mixed together and drawn at random to compile this piece and to create an interesting use of syntax.

"As a Matter of Fact," "The Misuse of Hostile Acts," "A Woman's Touch," "I Choose a Life of Style," "Textbook Thoughts Escape," "A Series of Three" and "Gold-plated Dreams" are all erasure poems inspired by *The Elements Of Style* by William Strunk Jr. and E.B. White, where I use the dry grammar text to create rich poetry.

"Breakfast, Lunch and Dinner" was written for the *CV2* 2014 2 Day Poetry Contest.

"Uganda 1972" was inspired by reading the history book *Idi Amin Dada: Hitler in Africa* by Thomas and Margaret Melady.

"Turning 19 In Vancouver" and "The Home Team Advantage" are erasure poems written using words from a local brew pub craft beer menu.

"Heavens Open" was written as part of *Geist*'s 2013 Erasure
Poetry Contest using the source text from Rachel Lebowitz's
Cottonopolis.

"How to Run Your Fingers Through My Hair" was inspired
by the film *Hustle and Flow* and dedicated to the director,
Craig Brewer.